CONTENTS

Words in the glossary appear in **bold** type the first time they are used in the text.

FUN ON ICE

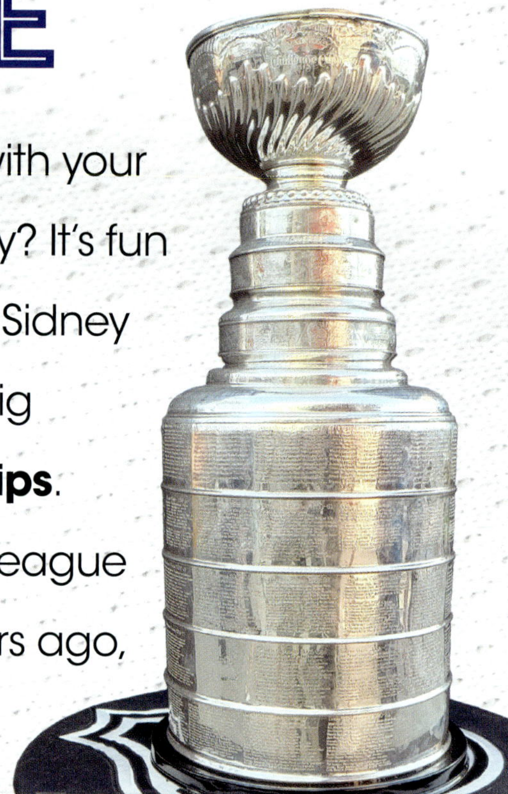

Do you like to play hockey with your friends on the ice or in a driveway? It's fun to pretend you're a superstar like Sidney Crosby or Patrick Kane, scoring big goals and winning **championships**.

Since the National Hockey League (NHL) began more than 100 years ago, *a lot* of great players have lifted the Stanley Cup. But the NHL isn't the only league for this sport's top players. Read on to learn about the amazing players and moments in this high-speed sport.

Get the Stats!

The Stanley Cup is the oldest sports trophy, or prize, in North America. It's also the only sports trophy on which every member of the championship team has their name listed.

Sports Stars, Stats, and Stories

HOCKEY STARS, STATS, AND STORIES

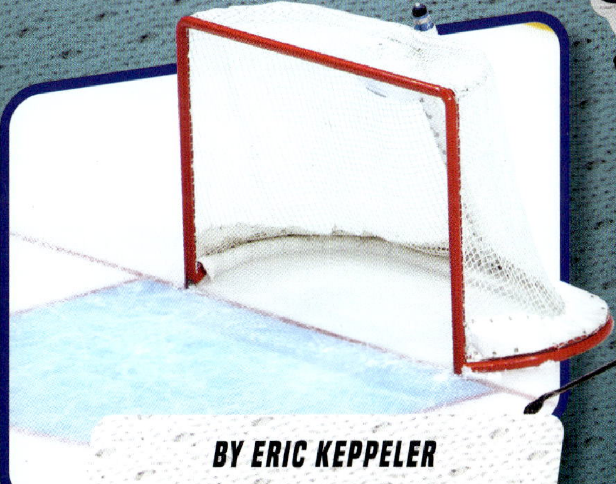

BY ERIC KEPPELER

Enslow PUBLISHING

INVESTIGATE!

Please visit our website, www.enslow.com. For a free color catalog of all our high-quality books, call toll free 1-800-398-2504 or fax 1-877-980-4454.

Library of Congress Cataloging-in-Publication Data
Names: Keppeler, Eric, author.
Title: Hockey stars, stats and stories / Eric Keppeler.
Description: Buffalo, New York : Enslow Publishing, 2025. | Series: Sports stars, stats, and stories | Includes index.
Identifiers: LCCN 2024033483 (print) | LCCN 2024033484 (ebook) | ISBN 9781978542617 (library binding) | ISBN 9781978542600 (paperback) | ISBN 9781978542624 (ebook)
Subjects: LCSH: Hockey players–Biography–Juvenile literature. | Hockey players–Statistics–Juvenile literature. | Hockey–Records–Juvenile literature. | Hockey–History–Juvenile literature.
Classification: LCC GV847.25 .K473 2025 (print) | LCC GV847.25 (ebook) | DDC 796.962–dc23
LC record available at https://lccn.loc.gov/2024033483
LC ebook record available at https://lccn.loc.gov/2024033484

Published in 2025 by
Enslow Publishing
2544 Clinton Street
Buffalo, NY 14224

First Edition

Designer: Andrea Davison-Bartolotta
Editor: Therese Shea

Photo credits: Cover, p. 1 (net) Gints Ivuskans/Shutterstock.com; cover (puck) mexrix/Shutterstock.com; cover, p. 1 (ref) A Santi Wajitdol/Shutterstock.com; cover (skates) forden/Shutterstock.com; cover, p. 1 (stick) Igor Sokolov (breeze)/Shutterstock.com; series art (banners) WinWin artlab/Shutterstock.com; series art (jersey texture) Kwangmoozaa/Shutterstock.com; series art (fact box background) Adam Vilimek/Shutterstock.com; series art (tablet) Lemberg Vector studio/Shutterstock.com; p. 4 Tino Bandito/ Shutterstock.com; p. 5 YES Market Media/Shutterstock.com; p. 6 meunierd/Shutterstock.com; p. 7 (hockey icon) Vector Vibes/ Shutterstock.com; p. 7 Håkan Dahlström/Flickr.com; p. 8 Mike W./Flickr.com; p. 9 (bottom) File:Gordie Howe Chex card.jpg/ Wikimedia Commons; p. 9 (top) Susan Montgomery/Shutterstock.com; p. 11 UPI Photo/Stephen Gross/Alamy Stock Photo; pp. 12, 13 Jai Agnish/Shutterstock.com; pp. 15 (both), 17 Iurii Osadchi/Shutterstock.com; p. 16 PixelSquid3d/Shutterstock.com; p. 19 Keith J Finks/Shutterstock.com; p. 20 UPI/Roger L. Wollenberg/Alamy Stock Photo; p. 21 (ice) mariakray/Shutterstock.com; p. 21 (Brodeur) Chip Griffin/Flickr.com; p. 21 (puck) pikepicture/Shutterstock.com; p. 23 PCN Photography/Alamy Stock Photo; p. 24 EWY Media/Shutterstock.com; p. 25 © ASSOCIATED PRESS; p. 26 (left) maniacduhockey/ File:Chandails rétirés CH, Plante, Moore, Harvey, M.Richard, Bouchard, Lach, Morenz.jpg/Wikimedia Commons; p. 26 (right) meunierd/Shutterstock.com; p. 27 (top) Michael Barera/File:HHOF July 2010 Canadiens locker 15 (Plante).JPG/Wikimedia Commons; p. 27 (bottom) Bibliothèque et Archives nationales du Québec; p. 28 Oleksandr Osipov/Shutterstock.com; p. 29 BDZ Sports/File:HilaryKnight.jpg/Wikimedia Commons.

Printed in the United States of America

CPSIA compliance information: Batch #CW25ENS: For further information contact Enslow Publishing, at 1-800-398-2504.

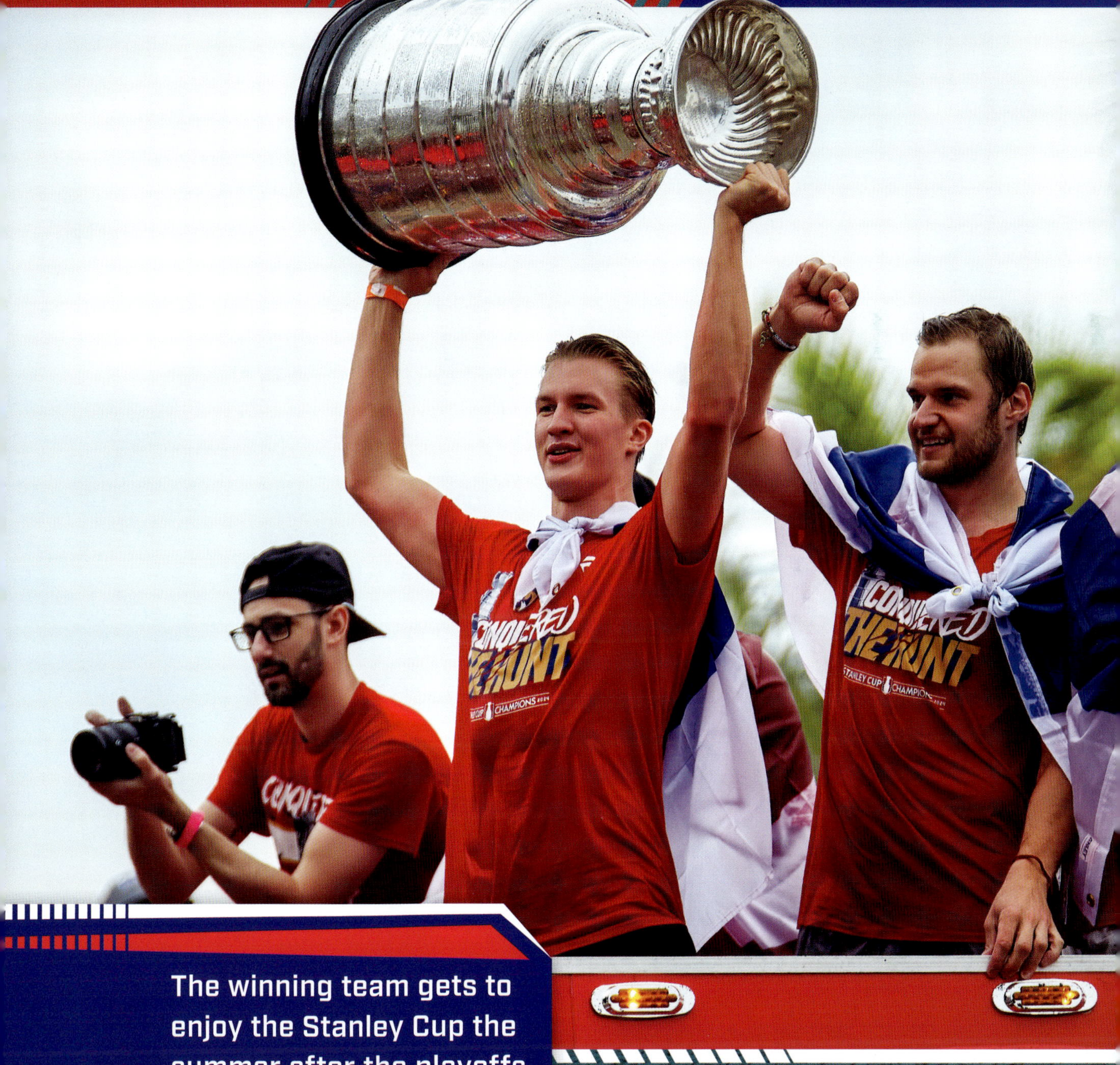

The winning team gets to enjoy the Stanley Cup the summer after the playoffs.

THE GREAT ONE

He's called the "Great One," so you know Wayne Gretzky is a star. Gretzky started his NHL **career** in 1979 with the Edmonton Oilers. As a center, he scored 51 goals and 86 assists in his first season! He won four Stanley Cups with the Oilers.

Gretzky was traded to the Los Angeles Kings in 1988 and played for the St. Louis Blues and New York Rangers too. When he retired, or stopped playing, in 1999, he held or shared 61 NHL records! Most still haven't been broken. He entered the Hockey Hall of Fame in 1999.

Gretzky not only scored goals, he helped others score too. In hockey, a player's number of points is the sum of their goals and assists. An assist is a point given to the player or players who pass the puck to the goal scorer.

GRETZKY'S TOP RECORDS

- most career goals: 894
- most career assists: 1,963
- most career points: 2,857
- most goals in one season: 92
- most points in one season: 215
- most assists in one season: 163
- most points in one playoff season: 47
- most career playoff points: 382

Wayne Gretzky has more career assists (1,963) than anyone else has total points.

Get the Stats!

Gretzky wore the number 99. The whole league retired that number in his honor. No other NHL player will ever wear it.

RED HOT WING

Gordie Howe had the most goals in NHL history (801) until Gretzky broke that record. Nicknamed "Mr. Hockey," Howe played 25 seasons with the Detroit Red Wings and led them to four Stanley Cup championships (1950, 1952, 1954, and 1955). A right wing, he led the league in scoring six times. Howe won the Hart Memorial Trophy for the league's most valuable player (MVP) six times too.

Howe also got into many fights on the ice. Today, a "Gordie Howe **hat trick**" is when a player has a goal, assist, and fight in the same game.

HART MEMORIAL TROPHY

With his success, Gordie Howe helped the city of Detroit, Michigan, earn the nickname "Hockeytown."

Get the Stats!

At age 51, Gordie Howe played his last NHL season in 1979 with his sons Mark and Marty on the Hartford Whalers.

SUPER MARIO

Mario "Super Mario" Lemieux played for the Pittsburgh Penguins between 1984 and 2005. He had a lot of health problems but still became one of the best goal scorers in history.

Lemieux first retired in 1997 because he had a **cancer** called Hodgkin lymphoma. He began to play again three years later but retired for good in 2006 due to heart problems. In 17 seasons, he led the Penguins to two Stanley Cups, in 1991 and 1992, and scored 690 career goals.

Get the Stats!

In 1999, Lemieux and others bought the Penguins, who were in financial trouble, saving the team from moving to another city. So, he was a player and owner at the same time.

Mario Lemieux, a center, often led the league in average points per game. His career points per game are 1.88, second only to Wayne Gretzky. Some wonder what records Lemieux might have broken if he had remained healthy.

THE GREAT 8

Russian Alexander Ovechkin has received a lot of attention over the years for his goal scoring. Nicknamed the "Great 8," Ovechkin is a three-time NHL MVP. He helped his Washington Capitals win its first Stanley Cup in 2018. He also holds records for most overtime goals and most **power play** goals, and he's tied with Mike Bossy and Wayne Gretzky for most 50-goal seasons, at nine.

After the 2023–2024 season, at age 38, Ovechkin had 853 career goals—just 41 shy of Gretzky's record of 894.

Ovechkin entered the NHL in 2005, the same year as superstar center Sidney Crosby of the Pittsburgh Penguins. Ovechkin won the Calder Memorial Trophy for **rookie** of the year. He had 106 points, while Crosby had 102.

Get the Stats!

Ovechkin, a left wing, has led the league in goals a record nine times.

GREATS OF WOMEN'S HOCKEY

Hayley Wickenheiser led Team Canada to four **Olympic** gold medals, twice as MVP. She also won seven gold medals and four silver at the IIHF (International Ice Hockey Federation) World Women's Championships. Wickenheiser retired in 2017 with a Team Canada record 168 goals.

Cammi Granato was the first woman to enter the Hockey Hall of Fame. She played on the first U.S. women's national team as a center and right wing. As captain, she led the Americans to gold in the 1998 Olympics. She is Team USA's all-time scoring leader with 343 points.

Many consider Hayley Wickenheiser, who played as center, the greatest female hockey player. In 2022, she became an assistant general manager with the Toronto Maple Leafs.

Forward Kendall Coyne Schofield is one of the most successful American women's hockey players. As a member of Team USA, she won six World Women's Championships and three Olympic medals—one gold and two silver.

In 2019, Coyne Schofield was invited to take part in the NHL All-Star Game skills contest for fastest skater. She finished less than a second behind the winner, Edmonton's Connor McDavid. In 2024, she began to play for Minnesota in the newly founded Professional Women's Hockey League.

Get the Stats!

Coyne Schofield did voice work for the 2024 movie* Inside Out 2*, playing the part of a hockey announcer.

As of 2024, Kendall Coyne Schofield has scored 82 goals and 186 points in 184 games for Team USA.

KENDALL COYNE SCHOFIELD

TOP DEFENDERS

Bobby Orr is often called the best **defenseman** ever because he was a great defender and scorer. He had 915 points in just 657 career regular-season games. Orr led the Boston Bruins to two Stanley Cups, in 1970 and 1972. He was named the NHL's best defenseman a record eight times—eight years in a row!

Ray Bourque holds the record for most points by a defenseman with 1,612. Defenseman Nicklas Lidström set a record in his last year in 2011, playing in 900 winning games.

Get the Stats!

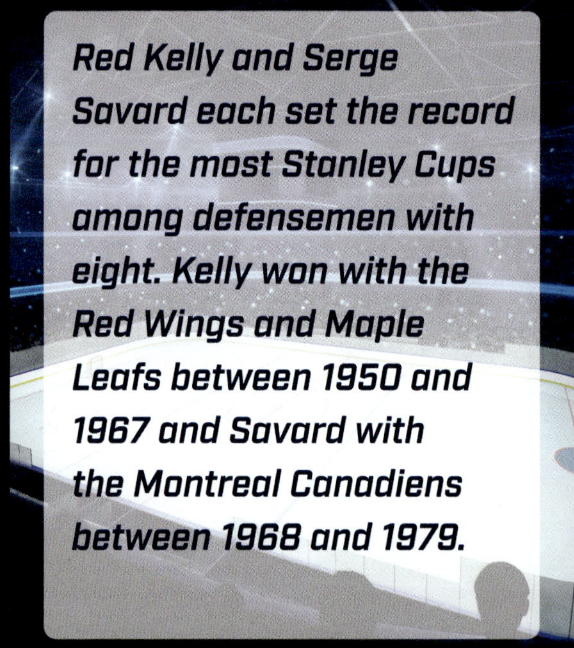

Red Kelly and Serge Savard each set the record for the most Stanley Cups among defensemen with eight. Kelly won with the Red Wings and Maple Leafs between 1950 and 1967 and Savard with the Montreal Canadiens between 1968 and 1979.

This statue in Boston shows Bobby Orr flying through the air after scoring the Stanley Cup-winning goal in 1970.

GOALIE GREAT

Martin Brodeur is considered one of the best goaltenders ever. He won the Calder trophy for rookie of the year in 1994 with New Jersey and helped the Devils win their first Stanley Cup one year later. He led the Devils to two more Stanley Cup wins in 2000 and 2003 and became the league's all-time goalie leader in wins (691) before he retired in 2015.

Brodeur also played in the Olympics for Team Canada four times. He won gold in 2002 and 2010. He entered the Hockey Hall of Fame in 2018.

MARTIN BRODEUR (LEFT), ROBERTO LUONGO (RIGHT)

BRODEUR'S
Goaltending Records

most regular season games played: 1,266

most regular season wins: 691

most regular season **shutouts**: 125

most playoff shutouts: 24

most 40-win seasons: 8

Martin Brodeur is now a vice president of hockey operations with the Devils.

AND THE GOALIE SCORES!

Nobody expects goalies to score goals–but it's happened! In 1979, Billy Smith of the New York Islanders was the first goalie to be credited with a goal, though it was an "own goal," or a goal scored by a team into their own net by accident.

Ron Hextall of the Philadelphia Flyers got the first of his two **empty-net** goals in 1987. Martin Brodeur has three goals on his record! As of 2023, 14 goalies have been credited with 17 goals.

Get the Stats!

Only seven goalies have won the Hart MVP award. Dominick Hasek is the only one who has won it twice, in 1997 and 1998, when he was with the Buffalo Sabres.

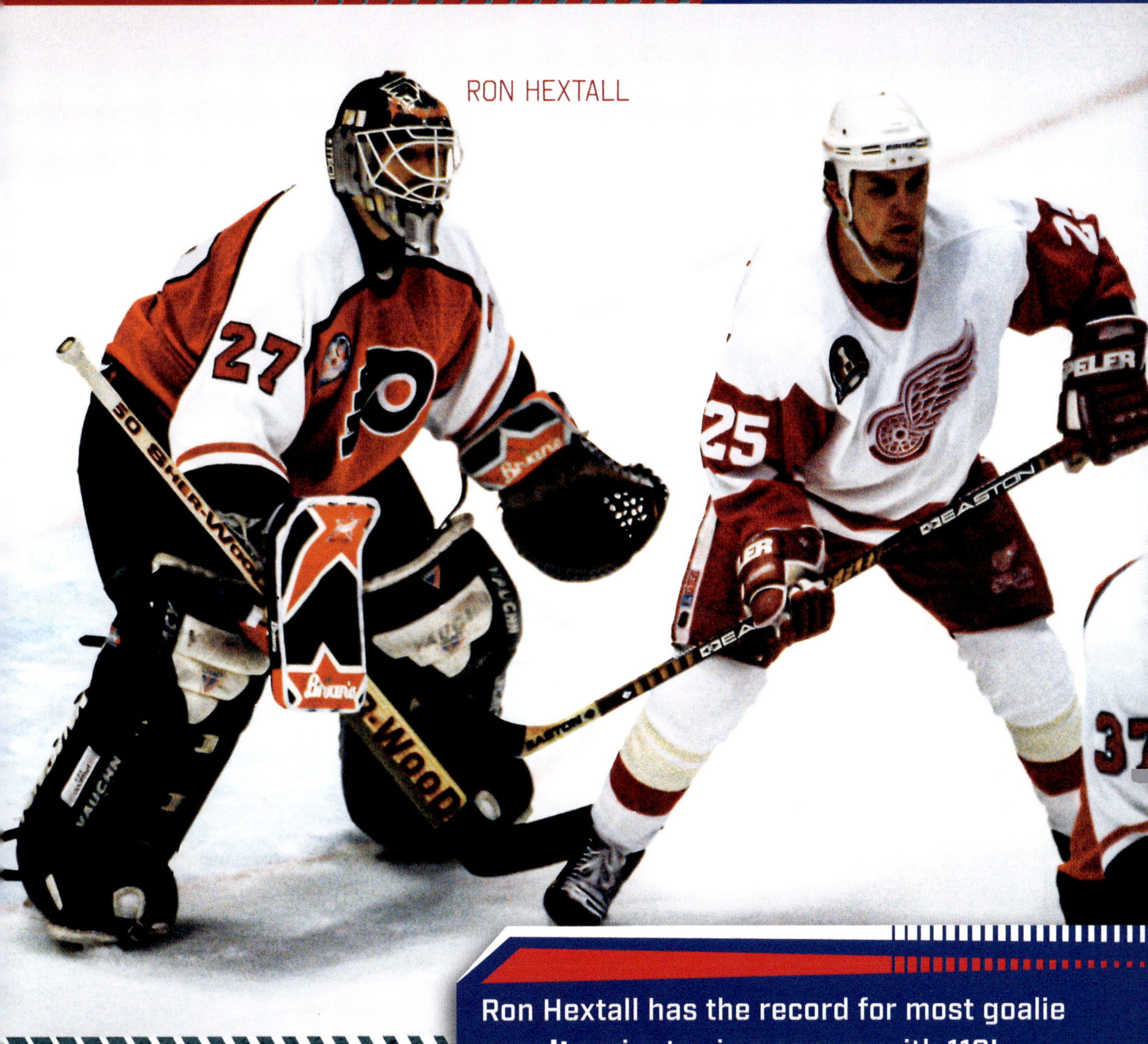

RON HEXTALL

Ron Hextall has the record for most goalie **penalty** minutes in a season with 113!

MIRACLE ON ICE

The U.S. men's national hockey team scored one of the greatest sports upsets at the 1980 Olympics. They faced off against a powerful Soviet Union team in the **semifinals**.

At that time, no pros were allowed in the Olympics. The Soviet players were highly trained, but the U.S. team, led by coach Herb Brooks, was made up of young college players. They weren't expected to win. However, Team USA managed to get—and keep—the lead in the third period against the Soviets. The game came to be known as the **Miracle** on Ice.

HERB BROOKS STATUE

The U.S. men's hockey team went on to win the gold medal against Finland in the final. Many players later had NHL careers.

TOP TEAM?

The Montreal Canadiens have won the Stanley Cup a record 24 times. Canadiens goalies Jacques Plante and Ken Dryden both won six Stanley Cups. Maurice "Rocket" Richard was the first NHL player to score 50 goals in one season (1944–1945). And Guy LaFleur, Jean Beliveau, and Henri Richard all scored more than 1,000 points for the Canadiens.

Some think the 1976–1977 team was the best of all. Their record was 60 wins, 8 losses, and 12 ties on the way to a Stanley Cup win. They had nine future Hall of Famers!

In 1959, Jacques Plante became the first goalie to wear a mask for safety and never played without it again.

MAURICE "ROCKET" RICHARD

Get the Stats!

The Maurice "Rocket" Richard Trophy is presented yearly to the goal-scoring leader during the regular season.

STARS OF TODAY AND TOMORROW

The great hockey players of today are wowing crowds. NHL stars such as Connor McDavid and Nathan MacKinnon and PWHL standouts such as Marie-Philip Poulin and Hilary Knight are likely headed for the Hall of Fame.

Every year, men's and women's pro leagues welcome talented young men and women. Most of these players got their start on youth teams when they were very young. The next great hockey star is playing youth hockey right now. Maybe it's you!

Get the Stats!

The USA Hockey organization reported 387,910 youth hockey players in 2022–2023, including about 70,000 girls.

Hilary Knight won the first IIHF Female Player of the Year award in 2023.

GLOSSARY

cancer: A disease caused by the uncontrolled growth of cells in the body.

career: The whole amount of time someone spends at a job.

championship: Events that decide the overall winner of a sport or contest.

defenseman: A player skilled at stopping other players from scoring.

empty net: In hockey, when a team removes their goaltender from the ice.

hat trick: In hockey, when three goals are scored by one player in a game.

miracle: A very surprising event that isn't expected to occur.

Olympic: Having to do with the Olympic Games, an international sports competition held once every two years, switching back and forth between summer and winter games.

penalty: A punishment for breaking a rule of a game.

power play: In hockey, when one team has more players on the ice than the other team for an amount of time because of a penalty.

rookie: A player during their first year in the league.

semifinal: A game or games to decide which teams will be in the final part of a competition or tournament.

shutout: A game in which no points are scored by the other team.

FOR MORE INFORMATION

BOOKS

Berglund, Bruce. *Hockey Records Smashed!* North Mankato, MN: Capstone Press, 2024.

Flynn, Brendan. *Hockey*. Minneapolis, MN: A & D Xtreme, 2023.

Kenan, Tessa. *Hockey*. Minneapolis, MN: Jump!, 2022.

WEBSITES

The Hockey Hall of Fame
www.hhof.com
This is the official site of the Hockey Hall of Fame, located in Toronto, Canada.

The 100 Greatest Players of the NHL'S First 100 Years
www.nhl.com/fans/nhl-centennial/100-greatest-nhl-players
The NHL's official website lists and explains this selection of the top 100 players so far.

The Professional Women's Hockey League
www.thepwhl.com/en/
Learn more about this league, which has teams in the United States and Canada.

INDEX